# YOU KNOW YOU'RE FROM CHCH WHEN...

Volume 2

To the wonderful people of Christchurch and Canterbury
and to the thousands of contributors to the YKYFCW Facebook page.

## On 4 September 2010 Canterbury was rocked by a 7.1 magnitude earthquake. Almost six months later, on 22 February 2011, a second major quake struck.

Although technically an aftershock to the September earthquake, its epicentre was closer to Christchurch, and shallower, and the devastation was unimaginably more catastrophic. With the city centre in ruins, suburbs and outlying areas destroyed, and with a sickening loss of life and injury, a grieving Canterbury was once again brought to its knees.

Two years on from the September earthquake, much of the central city is still cordoned off. The task of demolishing damaged buildings has begun, and it may be many months — even years — until rebuilding can begin. But in true red-and-black spirit, Cantabrians have picked themselves up and started to rebuild their homes and lives.

After the February earthquake, Bruce Raines's YKYFCW Facebook page became an instant sensation and a lifeline for many of those affected by the earthquake, and it's still going strong. Over $17,000 has been donated to the Christchurch Earthquake Mayoral Relief Fund from proceeds of the first YKYFCW book. *You Know You're From Christchurch When … Volume 2* celebrates Cantabrians' unremitting capacity for finding humour in the darkest of times.

# YOU KNOW YOU'RE FROM CHCH WHEN…

Every day is a leap day.

You get ready for winter by filling the cracks in your house with expanding foam to make it weathertight.

YOU
KNOW
YOU'RE
FROM
CHCH
WHEN...

YOU
KNOW
YOU'RE
FROM
CHCH WHEN...

Half your photos have wire netting
in front of them.

Erectile dysfunction is a problem with buildings.

YOU
KNOW
YOU'RE
FROM
CHCH WHEN...

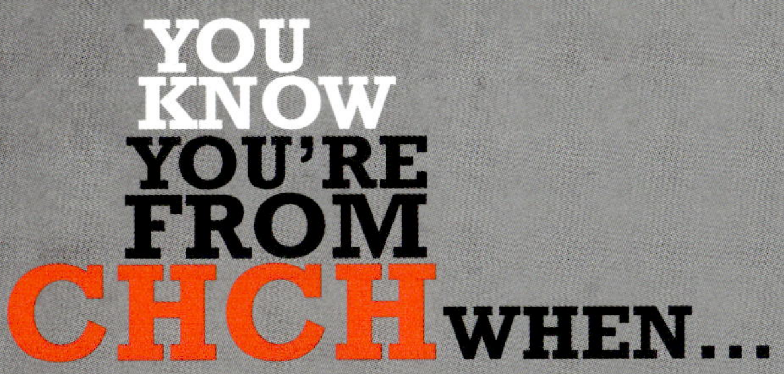
YOU
KNOW
YOU'RE
FROM
CHCH WHEN...

Road cones are more popular to decorate than Christmas trees.

YKYFCW becomes
a household name.

YOU
KNOW
YOU'RE
FROM
CHCH WHEN...

YOU KNOW YOU'RE FROM CHCH WHEN...

The only things on your shelves are unwanted gifts.

You've become so used to your munted things, they don't seem munted any more.

YOU
KNOW
YOU'RE
FROM
CHCH WHEN...

YOU
KNOW
YOU'RE
FROM
CHCH WHEN...

Demolition has become a spectator sport.

2

You and all your friends and family become characters in a living documentary.

YOU KNOW
YOU'RE
FROM
CHCH WHEN...

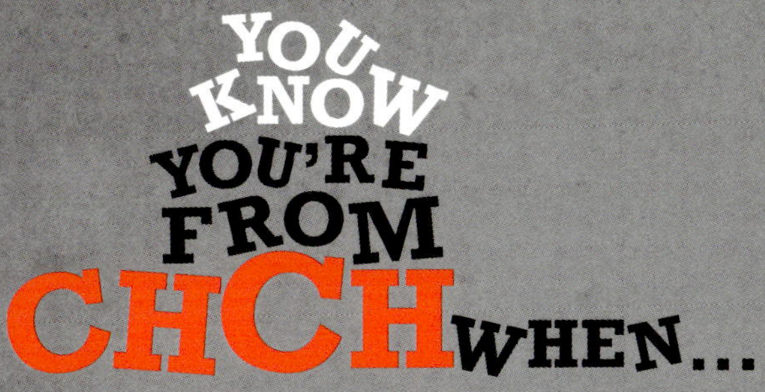
YOU KNOW YOU'RE FROM CHCH WHEN...

You can't decide if your friends and family have quake-brain, shake-brain or snow-brain.

Quake-brain means trying to look up Melbourne's shake on GeoNet.

YOU KNOW
YOU'RE FROM
CHCH WHEN...

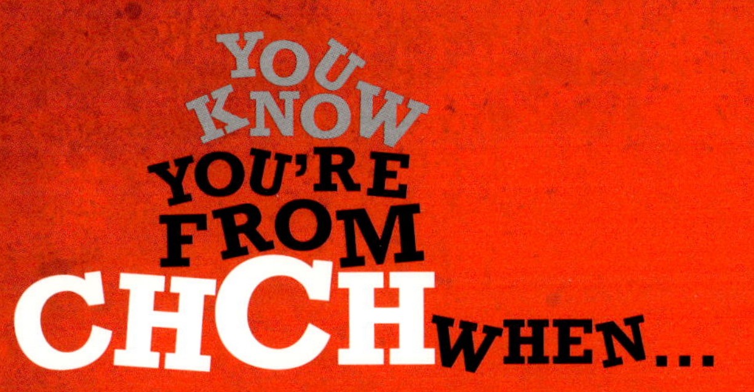
YOU KNOW YOU'RE FROM CHCH WHEN...

The only straight wall you have is on Facebook.

Police abandon a high-speed chase after the offending vehicle is clocked at 49 km/h. Police are confident they will track down the offenders because during the chase they leave behind their bumper, number plate, left rear door, exhaust system, $1.20 in coins, and a VIP discount wheel alignment card.

YOU KNOW YOU'RE FROM CHCH WHEN...

YOU KNOW
YOU'RE
FROM
CHCH WHEN...

Rangiora now has rush hour traffic.

You have QIACOBADS:
Quake Induced Advanced Crack
Or Bump Avoidance Driving Skills.

YOU
KNOW
YOU'RE
FROM
CHCH WHEN...

YOU KNOW YOU'RE FROM CHCH WHEN...

Your quake-brain makes you stock up on 'essentials' like twelve pots of Vicks VapoRub, which looked like a good deal on Trade Me.

2

Judder bars give you flashbacks.

YOU KNOW
YOU'RE
FROM
CHCH WHEN...

YOU KNOW YOU'RE FROM CHCH WHEN...

You're impressed with the road quality out in the rural parts of Christchurch.

You now have heaps of 'back in my day' comments ready for your future grandchildren.

YOU KNOW
YOU'RE
FROM
CHCH WHEN...

YOU KNOW
YOU'RE
FROM
CHCH WHEN...

Your chemistry teacher says, 'Water is odourless.' You reply, 'Not in Christchurch it isn't.'

You turn to YKYFCW as your one-stop site for the latest in news, sport, weather, DIY, self-help and humour.

YOU KNOW
YOU'RE FROM
CHCH
WHEN...

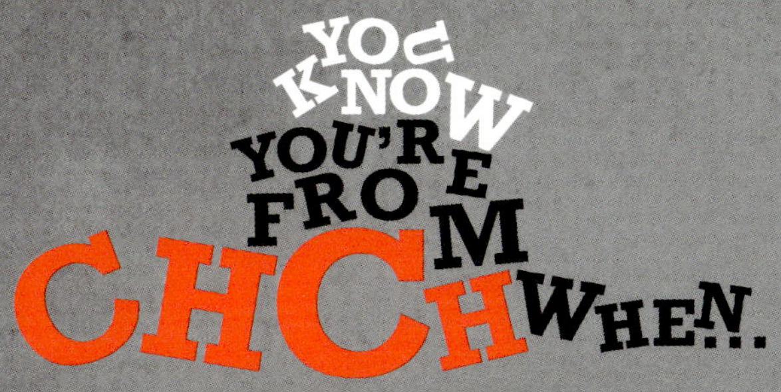
YOU KNOW YOU'RE FROM CHCH WHEN...

You see tall people in short cars shimmying down in the seat when driving.

Hi-vis attire makes
you feel at home.

YOU KNOW
YOU'RE FROM
CHCH WHEN...

YOU KNOW
YOU'RE FROM
CHCH WHEN...

Hard hats and reflective vests
are high fashion.

2

Even the locals can't give directions to tourists.

YOU KNOW YOU'RE FROM CHCH WHEN...

YOU KNOW
YOU'RE
FROM
CHCH
WHEN...

'5+ a day' has nothing to do with fruit and veg.

The water smells like a pool,
the supermarket smells like a pub,
and the street smells like a loo.

YOU KNOW
YOU'RE
FROM
CHCH
WHEN...

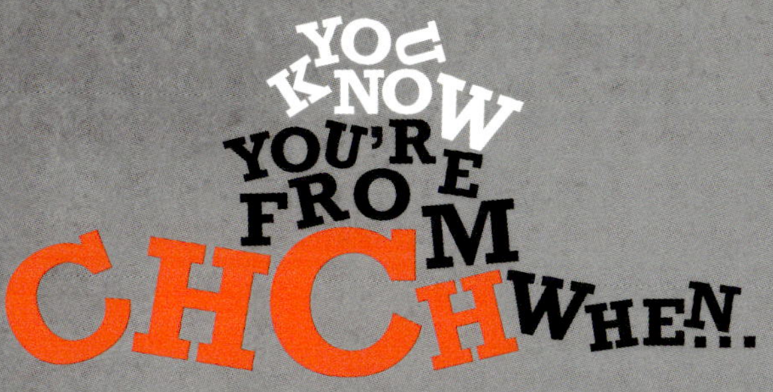
YOU KNOW YOU'RE FROM CHCH WHEN...

You buy your six-year-old Lego and the first thing he builds is a port-a-loo for his Lego men in case there's another earthquake.

You say, ‘We’ve only had twenty-seven shakes this week.’

YOU KNOW
YOU'RE FROM
CHCH WHEN...

YOU KNOW
YOU'RE FROM
CHCH WHEN…

It's fine to leave the house without using the toilet — there will be plenty along the way.

You drive past a dairy in a cargo container.

YOU KNOW
YOU'RE FROM
CHCH WHEN...

YOU'RE FROM CHCH WHEN...

You automatically grab your smartphone or laptop after a shake so you can check if you guessed the magnitude correctly.

You can choose to wash your 4x4 or just drive it through the flooded road near your house.

YOU KNOW
YOU'RE FROM
CHCH WHEN...

You know you're from CHCH when...

You know an online auction for a port-a-loo is going to spark a bidding war.

The CBD has more car parks than cars.

YOU'RE FROM CHCH WHEN...
YOU KNOW

YOU KNOW YOU'RE FROM CHCH WHEN...

You get stuck in moving-house traffic at 10 p.m. on a Wednesday.

There are roads
in the potholes.

YOU KNOW
YOU'RE FROM
CHCH WHEN...

YOU KNOW
YOU'RE FROM CHCH WHEN...

Facebook usage goes down thirty per cent due to lack of large aftershocks.

You arrange your dining room chairs in such a way that you can easily dive under the table.

YOU KNOW
YOU'RE FROM
CHCH
WHEN...

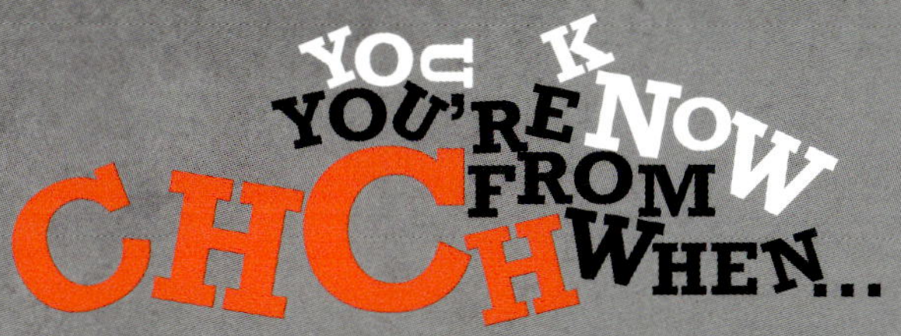
YOU KNOW
YOU'RE FROM
CHCH WHEN...

You ask, ‘What suburb do you live in?’
‘Suburb?’
‘Oh, sorry, I mean zone.’

You wish a six-pointer was a shark
or at least a style of car parking.

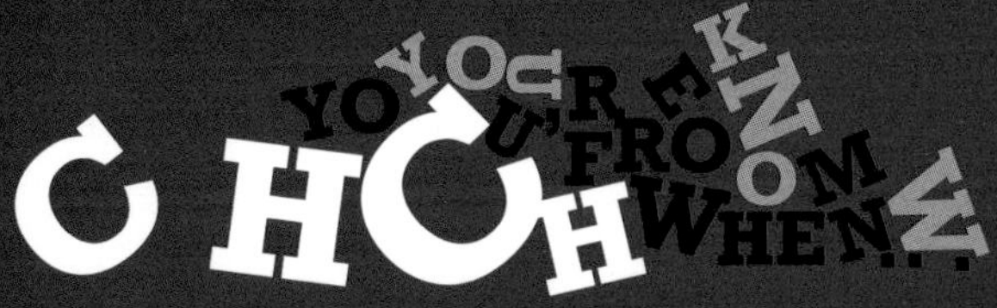
YOU KNOW YOU'RE FROM CHCH WHEN...

A staple diet is your food stapled to a shelf, table, bench or whatever it might fall off.

Occupying the CBD is impossible.

You turn your music up loud so your neighbour across the road with no power can hear it.

Your nightly prayer goes:
'Now I lay me down to rest,
I pray my house will stand the test.
If it should shake before I wake,
I pray the big TV won't break.'

You know you're from Christchurch when...

You can make a hilarious joke
before a major earthquake
has even finished.

A psychologist suggests Cantabrians must do the following things to reduce stress: 1. Get a good night's sleep *(how the hell do we do that with aftershocks?)* 2. Reduce alcohol *(I would if the aftershocks stop)* 3. Eat well *(between drinks?)* 4. Do something pleasurable *(drink alcohol)*.

YOU KNOW YOU'RE FROM
CHCH
WHEN...

You used to go into Christchurch for a custard square — now the whole square is custard.

2

It snows and you smile at the irony. Now we are trucking loads of sand back *in* to the city.

YOU KNOW
YOU'RE FROM
CHCH
WHEN...

Someone moving to Christchurch makes the front-page news.

There's no longer a problem finding a parking spot in town, as long as your car can get over the kerb.

YOU KNOW YOU'RE FROM
CHCH WHEN. . .

You want an aftershock
so the snow will fall out of your
satellite dish and you can
watch Sky TV again.

2

You get a safety demonstration
from the flight attendants …
as you get *off* the plane.

YOU KNOW YOU'RE FROM CHCH WHEN...

The 'Footpath closed, please use other side' sign really means, 'Footpath is in the river, you have no choice but to use the other side'.

Christchurch has had three earthquakes in 24 hours at 4.0 and over, and it doesn't even rate a mention on Facebook.

Oh, how times change.

YOU KNOW YOU'RE FROM
CHCH WHEN. . .

GeoNet has been checked every day for 365 days.

Saying you can't find a car park in the CBD now means the entire parking building.

YOU KNOW YOU'RE FROM CHCH WHEN...

YOU KNOW YOU'RE FROM
CHCH WHEN. . .

You need to wear a sports bra
while driving your car.

In case of an earthquake you make jelly. (It's fun to watch.)

YOU KNOW YOU'RE FROM CHCH WHEN . . .

YOU KNOW YOU'RE FROM CHCH WHEN...

You update your house's GPS location more frequently than you change the clocks.

You and your spouse find yourselves holding on to each other and jumping for joy in the driveway on a Saturday evening, not because you won Lotto, but because someone has finally fixed the drains.

YOU'RE FROM CHCH WHEN...
YOU KNOW

You know how to make a cocktail.
Simply add ingredients and wait.

You call the AA and they call back asking for directions through the road blocks.

YOU KNOW YOU'RE FROM CHCH WHEN...

You pick up your three-year-old from preschool and he tells you that he and his friends have been playing 'EQC'.

You feel completely ripped off when you get woken up at 2.22 a.m. by a 3.3 earthquake, when you now live in Adelaide.

YOU KNOW YOU'RE FROM CHCH WHEN...

YOU KNOW YOU'RE FROM CHCH WHEN...

Predictive text on your cellphone automatically enters 'aftershock'.

You wait to see if any of the comments you post on the YKYFCW Facebook page make it into the book.

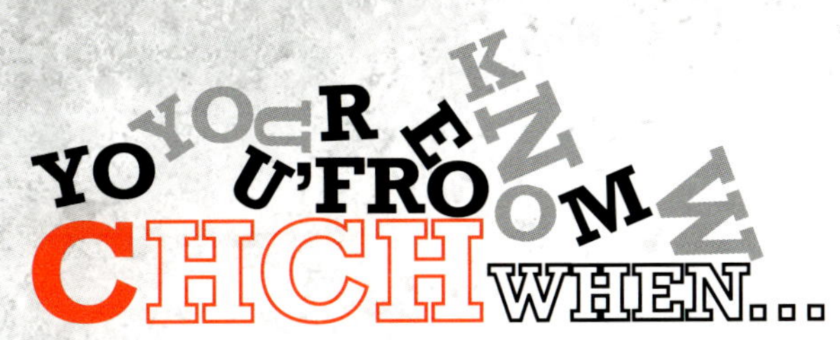
YOU KNOW YOU'RE FROM
CHCH WHEN...

Random hugging is normal.

Your countdown to the New Year is
5.1 … 4.8 … 4.3 …

YOU KNOW YOU'RE FROM
CHCH WHEN...

Your checklist for going to bed is:

Torch ✓

Teddy bear ✓

Extra pair of undies ✓✓

Anxiety tablets ✓✓✓✓✓✓✓

You no longer use the vibrate feature on your cellphone.

YOU KNOW
YOU'RE
FROM
CHCH
WHEN...

YOU KNOW
YOU'RE FROM
CHCH WHEN...

Anything above a magnitude 5.0
is a calorie burner.

You decorate road cones at Christmas, and New Year's is celebrated with a midnight shake.

YOU KNOW
YOU'RE
FROM
CHCH WHEN...

YOU'RE
YOU KNOW
FROM
CHCH
WHEN...

Visitors are considered baptized upon their first shake.

CERA releases findings of a survey of eastern suburbs residents. Apparently they are like dwarves: six out of seven are not Happy.

YOU KNOW
YOU'RE
FROM
CHCH
WHEN...

YOU KNOW
YOU'RE
FROM
CHCH WHEN...

You can rate shakes by YKYFCW members' posts and not by an official government website.

A 4.3 is disappointing.

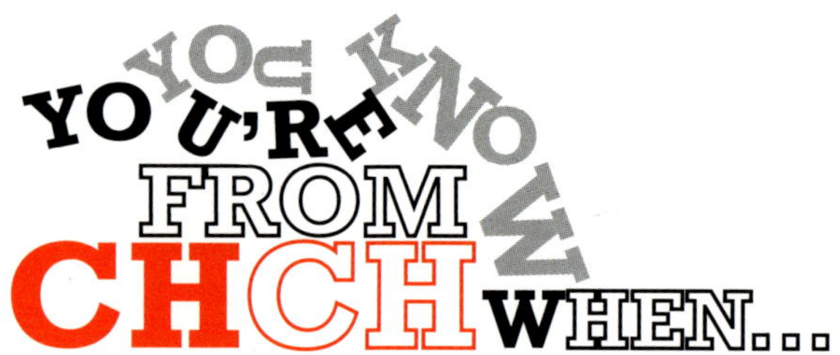
YOU'RE
YOU KNOW
FROM
CHCH WHEN...

YOU KNOW
YOU'RE
FROM
CHCH WHEN...

Coming from a broken home is even more normal than it used to be.

Blu-tack is a regular item on your shopping list.

YOU KNOW
YOU'RE
FROM
CHCH
WHEN...

YOU'RE
YOU KNOW
FROM
CHCH
WHEN...

Housework seems like
a waste of time.

Someone steals your gumboots instead of shoes.

YOU KNOW
YOU'RE
FROM
CHCH
WHEN...

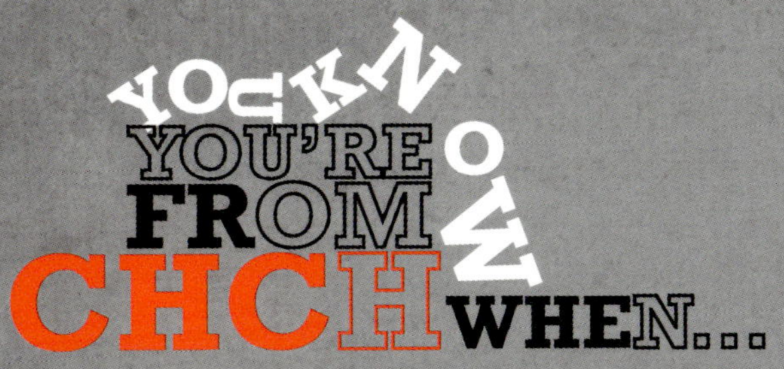
YOU KNOW
YOU'RE
FROM
CHCH WHEN...

You have lost interest in replying when asked 'Did you feel the earthquake?'

You go away for a holiday and decide which houses would be destroyed or red/green/yellow stickered after an earthquake.

YOU KNOW
YOU'RE
FROM
CHCH
WHEN...

YOU KNOW
YOU'RE
FROM
CHCH
WHEN...

You no longer get hay fever,
you get silt fever.

You move away from Christchurch's earthquakes and Auckland's tornadoes, and realize that moving to Wellington makes perfect sense.

YOU KNOW
YOU'RE
FROM
CHCH
WHEN...

YOU KNOW
YOU'RE
FROM
CHCH WHEN...

You think aftershocks make efficient, but unreliable, alarm clocks.

You get two torches for Christmas.

YOU KNOW
YOU'RE
FROM
CHCH WHEN...

YOU KNOW
YOU'RE
FROM
CHCH WHEN...

You have a bath in your togs, just in case.

Your doctor prescribes you motion sickness tablets to be taken every 12 hours.

YOU KNOW
YOU'RE
FROM
CHCH
WHEN...

YOU KNOW
YOU'RE
FROM
CHCH WHEN...

Potters use liquefaction silt for art.

A shop assistant says, 'Have a safe day' as you leave rather than 'Have a good day'.

YOU
KNOW
YOU'RE
FROM
CHCH WHEN...

YOU
KNOW
YOU'RE
FROM
CHCH WHEN...

You write:
Dear Insurer, any chance you could add a 'same sh*t as last time' option on your claims page?

You hope to sit at the table,
not under it.

YOU
KNOW
YOU'RE
FROM
CHCH WHEN...

You
KNOW
YOU'RE
FROM
CHCH WHEN…

You see your neighbours holding on to each other for dear life, when a week ago they could have killed each other.

You give up on glass cups.

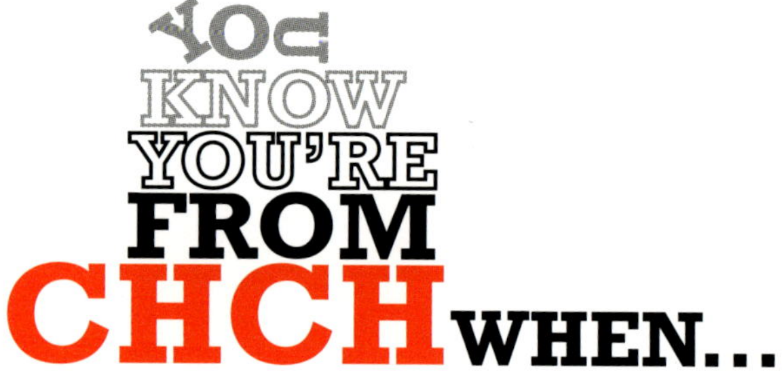
YOU
KNOW
YOU'RE
FROM
CHCH WHEN...

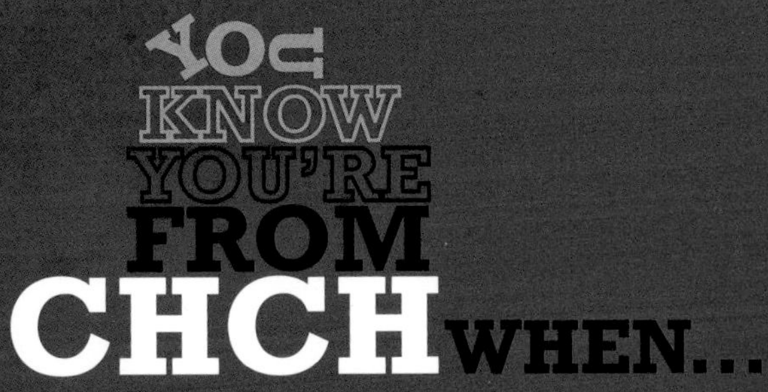
YOU
KNOW
YOU'RE
FROM
CHCH WHEN...

The boxing announcer yells,
'Let's get ready to rumble!'
and you dive under a table.

2

You wonder if that's a bit of eggshell in your pavlova or a piece of the ceiling.

YOU
KNOW
YOU'RE
FROM
CHCH WHEN...

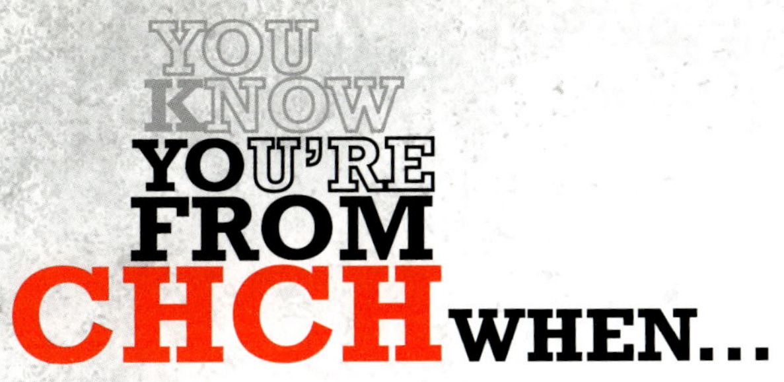
YOU
KNOW
YOU'RE
FROM
CHCH WHEN...

You think: Friday the thirteenth,
like Cantabs are scared of that.
Pfft!

The only number seven you want predicted is on a bottle of Jack Daniel's.

YOU
KNOW
YOU'RE
FROM
CHCH WHEN...

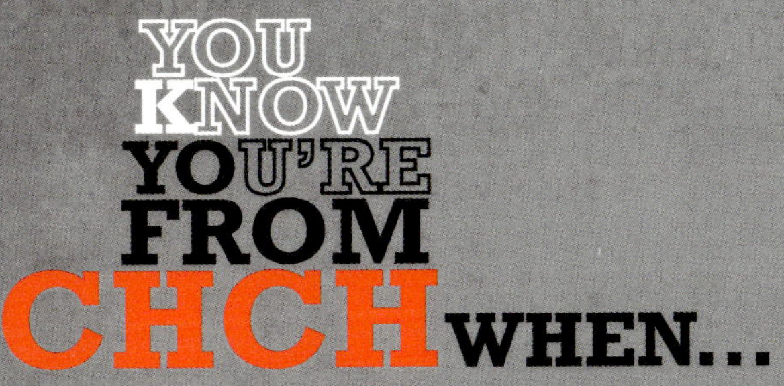
YOU
KNOW
YOU'RE
FROM
CHCH WHEN...

Supermarkets have Blu-tack for sale beside the sweets at checkouts.

Reaching 10,000 shakes is seen as a reason to open another beer.

YOU
KNOW
YOU'RE
FROM
CHCH WHEN...

YOU
KNOW
YOU'RE
FROM
CHCH WHEN...

You can Zumba while standing still.

February twenty-third is now considered Canterbury New Year by order of Mr Giggles.

YOU
KNOW
YOU'RE
FROM
CHCH WHEN...

YOU
KNOW
YOU'RE
FROM
CHCH WHEN...

You avoid the pothole that has been filled in for the umpteenth time, yet still it sinks down, and you wonder if, on the other side of the world, mounds of asphalt are appearing somewhere.

Your Marmite shortage nearly becomes a national emergency.

YOU
KNOW
YOU'RE
FROM
CHCH WHEN...

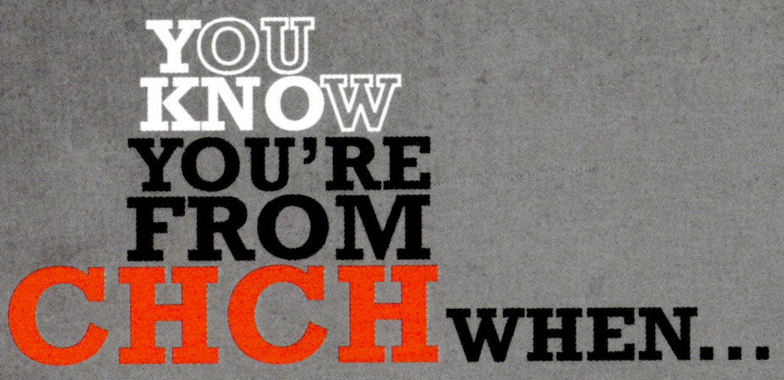
YOU
KNOW
YOU'RE
FROM
CHCH WHEN...

You consider buying a 4x4, but then think a hovercraft is a better option.

Fracking is a dirtier word than …
many others.

YOU
KNOW
YOU'RE
FROM
CHCH WHEN…

YOU KNOW YOU'RE FROM CHCH WHEN...

All your photographs have a port-a-loo in the background.

2

Your toddler names the streets based on earthquake references: Weeeeeee Road, Crack Road and Digger Road.

YOU
KNOW
YOU'RE
FROM
CHCH WHEN...

YOU
KNOW
YOU'RE
FROM
CHCH WHEN...

Visiting a friend's house in town gives you the jitters and a feeling of seasickness, and that's just from the trucks driving over the potholes too fast.

Your partner busting in on you in the shower gives you more of a fright than the 4.3 shake that prompted him.

YOU KNOW YOU'RE FROM CHCH WHEN...

YOU
KNOW
YOU'RE
FROM
CHCH WHEN...

You go to bed with your jacket within easy reaching distance and your cellphone charging in the pocket.

You make a quake humour book
and it becomes a bestseller.

YOU
KNOW
YOU'RE
FROM
CHCH WHEN...

This book has been designed and typeset by a Canterbury-based business. A percentage of the proceeds will be donated to the Red Cross New Zealand Earthquake Appeal.

**HarperCollins*Publishers***

First published 2012
HarperCollins*Publishers (New Zealand) Limited*
P.O. Box 1, Auckland 1140



**HarperCollins*Publishers***
31 View Road, Glenfield, Auckland 0627, New Zealand
Level 13, 201 Elizabeth Street, Sydney, NSW 2000, Australia
A 53, Sector 57, Noida, UP, India
77–85 Fulham Palace Road, London W6 8JB, United Kingdom
2 Bloor Street East, 20th Floor, Toronto, Ontario M4W 1A8, Canada
10 East 53rd Street, New York, NY 10022, USA

National Library of New Zealand Cataloguing-in-Publication Data
You know you're from Christchurch when--. Volume 2 / compiled
by Bruce Raines.
ISBN 978-1-86950-999-6
1. Earthquakes—Social aspects—New Zealand—Christchurch—Humor.
2. Canterbury Earthquake, N.Z., 2010—Humor. 3. New Zealand wit and
humor. 4. Christchurch (N.Z.)—Social life and customs—Humor.
I. Raines, Bruce.
363.3495099383—dc 23

ISBN: 978 1 86950 999 6
Cover design and typesetting by Book Design Ltd. www.bookdesign.co.nz
Printed by Geon, Auckland